Cedar Grove and Other Memories:

The Collected Works of Marjorie Beavers

By Marjorie Beavers

Edited by David and Jonathan Bennett

New Photographs by David Bennett

Compiled and Transcribed by Jennifer and Carmela Bennett

SECTIONS

SECTION I: WRITINGS   2

SECTION II: POEMS   43

ADDITIONAL PHOTOS   117

The author with her great granddaughter, Grace, in 2009

The author at Christmas 2007

~ Foreword ~

When my brother and I were young, small enough to play hide-and-go-seek in a laundry chute, I remember eagerly requesting to hear grandma's stories and poems. As we huddled around her, hanging on her every word, she would take us on stuffed-animal adventures in exciting settings, in which my brother and I were participants. We would also ask for more, and grandma would usually oblige, until every character was thoroughly developed, which was not easy, since the characters were made of fabric and stuffing.

The romantic poets remind us that words are not "just words," and that there is no such thing as "just a symbol." Words, phrases, symbols, and images do not just sit on a page, remaining neutral. They stimulate our senses, and evoke emotions, memories, and feelings.

This collection contains many such wonderful words and images, which detail my grandma's life in small-town Southern Ohio. Included are fictional stories, children's stories, poems, and general reflections on a variety of topics. These stories and poems reflect life as a loving wife, mother, grandmother, sister, and church and community member. They express the joys, wonder, and struggles of everyday life.

David Bennett
Cedar Grove Press, 2011

Section One: Writings

~ The Birth of Amelia ~

Amelia was a little checked bear. But for a long time, she was just a pattern on a piece of paper...waiting to be put together by loving hands.

One day she was placed in a big, dark mail bag and taken for a bumpy ride in the back of a truck. Her journey had begun! She was jostled this way and that way as the miles slowly passed by.

Suddenly the truck came to a stop beside a big, brick building, and the mail bags were carried inside. Amelia could hardly wait. Maybe now, at long last she was to be free. But no, once again she was put in a dark, scary place. This time it was a tiny mailbox. Then she heard a noise. She shivered in anticipation. A pair of hands picked her up, and once again she was on the move. This time she would surely find a place in someone's heart. Hurriedly, the envelope was torn open, and she heard a voice, "What a cute little bear." Then she was tucked away once more - high on a shelf.

For several days, she suffered in silence. When finally, it happened: the pattern was placed on a lovely checked cloth and little pins were stuck in it. "Ouch! that hurts." Snip, snip. Someone was cutting. "Oh, don't cut me!" Soon that frightening experience was over, but she still didn't feel like a real bear.

The sewing machine was now ready to do its work. Whirr, whirr it went as the needle moved up and down and around and around. Afterwards, her body was filled with some beautiful white fluffy stuffing.

"I have legs - and arms!" Happily she twiddled her little thumbs. Now two big button eyes were sewn on her face. She could surely see better. Then a nose, and a mouth. At last the birth pains were over and she was ready to live.

Oh, it seemed like days that Amelia stayed alone on that bed. Being a real bear wasn't so much fun after all. So back to sleep she went.

After hours of dreaming, she abruptly awoke. Strange and excited voices were coming near her. Her ears stuck straight out and her hair was standing on end. She just knew her life would be different from now on.

Closer and closer they came. She blinked her eyes for she thought she was seeing double. Coming toward her were two little boys looking just alike, and each carrying a fuzzy brown bear.

One bear spoke up. "My name is Puddin, and this is Badgy." "What's your name?"

"Why, I don't have a name," she sadly replied. Then, two arms reached out for her.

"Let's call her Amelia," they said, as she was carried from the room.

A shiny toy truck stood waiting and the bears were quickly placed inside. Amelia held tightly onto Puddin because she was a little afraid. Straight through the door they went.

Amelia had never, never, been outside. It was so big and bright! They stopped to smell some pretty spring flowers and climbed in the branches of the tall green trees. There were so many things to see and do. She hoped this day would never end.

Then back on the bed for a tired wee bear, but Amelia wasn't sad. She knew that another day would come when little arms would reach out for her.

Oh, the joy of being a real little bear, and the beginning of a new life for Amelia.

~ The Adventures of Amelia ~

Little twin boys, David and Jonathan, had a new friend, and her name was "Amelia." She was a little stuffed teddy bear and she longed to have a friend too. One day the boys brought their toy bears to grandma's house to play with Amelia.

They played as all little bears do and had a happy time, almost every day. They jumped on Grandma's bed, played hide-and-seek, and ate bread and honey. What fun they had! Suddenly the boys didn't come and bring their bears anymore. Their mommy and daddy had taken them on a vacation trip to the ocean where they could play on the beach.

Amelia was very sad and lonely, for she was left on the bed most of the day, and she became very bored.

One night when grandma was fast asleep, Amelia could be still no longer, so she quietly slipped from the bed. She was feeling very hungry - so into the kitchen she went. She could see a little light coming from the refrigerator. Luckily Grandma hadn't closed the door tightly. Amelia pulled and pulled. At last the door was open wide enough for a small bear to creep inside. "That jar of strawberry jam surely looks good," she said. Finally the lid was off and she put her paw inside. It sure tasted yummy! She sat down in a bowl of nice soft gravy left from Grandma's supper, and she ate and ate.

Back in the bedroom Grandma stretched and opened her eyes. She could hear a little noise coming from the kitchen. "Must be that mouse again," she said. "I'd better go set a trap."

Slowly she got up from the bed, rubbing her eyes, and went into the kitchen. Seeing the refrigerator door open, she stepped over to close it. "Amelia, what are you doing?" "Just look at you, all covered with Strawberry Jam!" "Into the washing machine with you young lady."

Soon the washing machine was filled with nice warm, soapy, water so Grandma tossed Amelia inside. At first Amelia thought it was fun as she bobbed about on the waves, but then she was tumbled upside down. Her eyes stung from the soap and her nose was filling with water. "Help I'm drowning!" "Just hold your nose," Grandma said. "I'll have you out in a minute." At last, she was wrapped in a nice warm towel. She was getting very sleepy. Grandma tucked her back into bed, and she snuggled among the covers and was soon fast asleep.

The next night Amelia could hardly wait for Grandma to close her eyes. She wanted to get into that big jar of honey on the kitchen shelf. Soon Grandma was snoring softly, so she crept into the kitchen. She was being ever so careful but suddenly there was a loud crash. She had knocked the jar onto the floor. Honey splattered everywhere!

Grandma jumped out of bed and ran into the kitchen. "Amelia, not you again?" "What am I going to do with you?" Amelia ran swiftly back to bed and hid among the covers. She knew Grandma was very angry.

After what seemed like hours of sweeping and mopping, the kitchen was clean once more, so Grandma climbed wearily back into bed.

When morning came Grandma heard the voices of the children. "We're home Grandma," they said. Then two arms reached out for Amelia. Grandma heaved a big sigh. Hopefully, the night adventures of Amelia had come to an end.

~ The Spirit of Christmas ~

As we entered the nursing home with Santa that cold winter night, very few were sitting around the glowing Christmas tree. Our "off pitch" singing was greeted with a smile, but just one or two tried to stumble over the words of the well-known Christmas carols.

Soon the white bearded Santa, dressed in his bright red suit, gave a little wink and began rummaging in his festive red and green bag. Out came a gaily wrapped gift especially picked for each one. A few soon tore off the wrappings, but others clutching them in their hands, slowly made their way back to their rooms, squeezing the gift and wondering what could be inside. Some would have no other packages to open, so perhaps they wanted to keep them and make the moment last. "What were they thinking?" Thoughts may have turned to happier times. A day when they were in their own homes with their loved ones gathered around, picturing each face; and the anticipation of gifts being opened with shouts of happiness. Later, a table filled with Christmas goodies for all to share, and heads bowed giving thanks to God for all his goodness. Wonderful memories of the past. The Spirit of Christmas had come!!!

We were almost ready to leave when my eyes were drawn as if by magic to one lone woman, who had appeared after the others had gone their way. She sat quietly holding her gift on her lap. Her face was alight with such a beautiful glowing smile, I found myself walking toward her. As I leaned over and clasped her hand, she told me she had no children, no brothers or sisters, no one; but I could tell God dwelt within her because of the radiance of her face. When she spoke, I could see she only had a tooth here and there, but that sweet smile hid all imperfections. It was a smile of beauty! She seemed so content, so loving, I felt she could have been an angel here only for a time, and if I returned she would be gone. Now, I know how it feels to be touched by an angel. The Spirit of Christmas had truly come!!

~ Old Age and a Computer (2005) ~

Getting a computer just a month after my eighty-first birthday was enough to cause goose bumps all over my body, and that was before it was even brought into the house. Knowing nothing whatsoever about a computer, I didn't know if I wanted that thing. When it was brought down and placed on my desk, it took a day or two just to get used to looking at it. I would just stare at it now and then. I don't know what I was expecting it to do.

Finally the big day came when I learned how to turn it on. That wasn't too hard, but doing something with it was another matter. I chased that little arrow all over the screen and it wouldn't go anywhere I wanted it to. After that little session, I was about ready to let my cat play with that mouse, to see if she could do any better.

Now the next lesson went a little easier. I finally could get that thing turned on and off. I was really learning. Oh boy!

Fortunately I could type a little, so was soon fascinated by my words on that tiny screen. Mistakes are a big part of my typing, but with help, I soon learned about those little keys to correct them. That was really something! I could erase a whole sentence and start over. Writing stories took on a whole new meaning, but sometimes that old computer wouldn't like some word that I had written. It would try its best to get me to change it. I don't see why it just didn't tell me exactly what it wanted me to say, instead of beating about the bush all the time. I was trying to write the memories of my early years and sometimes the right word wouldn't come. The computer seemed to know more about me than I did.

After several days, I did master writing a story, and would bring it up on the screen now and then, to read it, change some words, and make sure it made some sense.

One day, right in the middle of this, it suddenly stopped on me, and some rather frightening words flashed on the screen. "You have done something illegal." Wow! I finally decided it was best just to wait for the Sheriff to come, so I sat down and waited. I didn't know if needed a lawyer. Well, the Sheriff didn't show up, so I thought maybe I hadn't done anything bad after all. I went to my desk, turned my computer back on to see if it had any more bad news. I don't know what happened, but I was in the clear. I'll be more responsible for my actions after that episode.

Well so far, I haven't done much else except type. Haven't learned a thing new, and once in a while it still doesn't want to shut off. Boy, that thing has a mind of its own. I hope I'll be able to be the boss of this thing one of these days, but will keep a wary eye so as not to be caught in any wrongdoing.

Now just for a word of advice. If you want to be in complete control, maybe you should write in longhand. Could I be just too old to learn? Well, maybe, but I'm going to keep trying. I might even learn how to play solitaire. --Just remember, don't let your guard down.

~ A Cat And The Church (Oct. 2003) ~

It was a dark moonless night and Yeller was out for his nightly walk. Even with his cat eyes, he could see no mice to chase. And the friendly cat that lived next door was nowhere around, so he slowly sauntered up the street.

A big door stood open wide all aglow with light and warmth, just beckoning him to enter. Cautiously he looked inside. Nothing there to frighten him, so inside he went.

It was so big, with many rooms for a curious cat to investigate. He peered into each one, with ears alert to sounds which could possibly be a scurrying mouse.

After looking into each nook and cranny he ran up the winding stairs. Even a cat could tell of the beauty that was there. There was a wide aisle with many benches and a carpet of dazzling red. What a good place to play! But without a playmate he soon became tired of the game so he climbed up on a cushiony chair, curled up in a ball, and fell fast asleep.

Later a noise awakened him and he looked up in alarm. Perhaps he should go home. Down the stairs he ran, sometimes two or three steps at a time, but he could find no way to the outside. The door was tightly closed!

Poor Yeller was so scared and he would cry if only he could. Instead he let out a pitiful meow. His cries grew louder and louder until he was really yowling, but that didn't help to open the door.

Once again he ran up the stairs searching for a place of safety. Suddenly he spied an opening. Inside it was dark and a little scary, but he squeezed inside and hid behind a big board. Oh, how lonely he felt!

When morning came he crept from his hiding place. His stomach was so empty and he needed to go to the bathroom. He ran up the aisle and climbed up on the pews searching for something to eat. Then his nose caught the smell of food. Could that really be? He followed the smell and he soon had a little tummy full. Now he felt so much better but still lonely, so he crawled back in the dark hole to hide.

Sometime later he thought he heard his master's voice. Was he dreaming? But no, there it was again. He ran as fast as his little legs could carry him to the sound of that welcome voice. Warm loving hands picked him up, whispered words of love and carried him safely home.

In the nice warm kitchen he was given a big plate of food and then tenderly put on the living room couch. He could feel the love all around, and his loud purrs echoed the thanks he felt in his little heart.

~ A Look Back (2005) ~

I was born in a little house on a hillside, near Maysville, Kentucky, where the beautiful Ohio River could be seen in the distance. I have been told that my dad would sometimes swim over to the island in the middle of the river. He was a big strong man, about six feet tall and had brown wavy hair. He worked hard to provide for his family, and I know he had many hardships during his life, especially when he was a child.

I don't remember much about those early years, but know when we visited Mom's cousin in that area at a later time, we would sit on her big front porch and watch the paddle wheel boats and barges, usually carrying coal, go up and down the river. I faintly recall going on a show boat, where they put on old fashioned stage plays which was much needed entertainment for those who couldn't travel to the city.

We later moved to Vanceburg, Kentucky when Dad worked on the camp cars and he would often be away from home. Mom's sister, Hazel, lived nearby, which was nice for her. Then in 1927 or 28, Dad was given a job as Section Foreman on the C & O Railroad, not too far from Kingston. That's when we made the move to Ohio. Our furniture was loaded onto a boxcar and made the trip by rail, then our family made the journey by passenger train, as we didn't have an automobile at that time. Dad worked for the railroad for many years until his retirement when he reached 65 years of age.

I have many fond memories of Kingston, as it was when I was growing up, and I'm thankful to God that was in his plan for us. I know I'm a small town girl through and through, and I'm proud of it! I really enjoy living here, where you can walk on its peaceful streets and many times pause to greet an old friend.

I wish I could have a movie of the way it was back then. There were several grocery and dry goods stores, where you could buy anything from food to shoes, an elegant men's store for such a small town, a shoe repair shop, restaurants, and barber shops, where I'd go for haircut and tell the barber to cut my hair to the tips of my ears. He always kept a big board to put across the barber chair for the small fry to sit on.

There was also a jewelry store, hardware, bank, post office, and bakery among others. Sure different today. Everyone goes to the Malls now, and there are very few business places in Kingston. Many more people living here too, so it just isn't the same. Time sure marches on.

An old blacksmith shop was located about the center of town, and many of us walked on the path through the field on the way to school. There were farmers there most days with their big workhorses getting shod. We could see the fire and hear the clanging of the anvil, as the blacksmith did his work. We never realized then that it would soon be a thing of the past. The farmers would be using tractors and the workhorses would soon be just a memory. History was in the making!

That same field was the meeting place for the town teenagers on summer weekends for a game of softball, and at times there would be a circus or and old time medicine show, for young and old alike.

On many Saturday nights, farmers would come to town for their groceries, and in wintertime would sit around a stove at one end of the store, swap stories, and talk about the weather. Sometimes a family group would entertain with their guitars and sing the latest country songs, accompanied by some toe tapping from the loafers and the shoppers. No TV then, just pure live entertainment.

Roller Skating was so much fun back then too. All over town on sidewalks and up and down Pickaway Street we'd go, like we had wings and would soon take flight. My old friends Phyllis, Marvene, and I spent many an hour doing this. We'd meet some boys on Pickaway under the streetlight and pretend we were having church, although I doubt there was much religion in it.

In those days, my sister Ginny, had a paper route, but when she was able to find a job away from home, it was passed on to Pauline for a while, and then to me. I carried the Columbus Dispatch most of my high school years. I know the Sunday paper cost ten cents a copy, and it was a big heavy paper. I always had to have help then, and my sister Edna, would usually take part of my route, so we had to get up pretty early to get it to our customers before breakfast. It was a good way to earn spending money, but a little unpleasant when it was raining, or during the cold winds and blustery snows of winter.

After I graduated high school, I got a job at the village post office. We had mail that came in by train and dropped off at our little depot three times a day. At the same time, outgoing mail left Kingston. First class postage was three cents for a letter, and at Christmas time unsealed cards could be mailed for one and a half cents each. We had to cancel stamps manually and could get a pretty good rhythm going when we had a large number of letters to send out.

I didn't need an alarm clock while living at home and getting up early to go to work. I awoke each morning to the radio and the singing from the Cadle Tabernacle. There was preaching by Rev. Cadle and Mrs. Cadle, with her not so beautiful voice singing, "Ere You Left Your Room This Morning, Did You Think To Pray?" I can almost hear it now. It was on kind of loud, as

Mom would be in the kitchen fixing breakfast for Dad and packing his lunch bucket. I knew then it was time to start my day.

I worked at the post office six days a week, and for all the hours I spent there, I was paid twelve dollars every two weeks. After a time, another postal clerk left her job, so I was senior worker then, and I earned quite a bit more money. I always bought some nice clothes, and many times would go to Schachne's Dept. Store in Chillicothe, where I could buy my dress pumps for three dollars a pair, and pretty skirts and sweaters for about five dollars. It was always fun to shop there, and it was rather fascinating to watch the little money containers go back and forth on cables, from the sales ladies to the cashier, high in one end of the store. Even after shopping, I had some spending money, and sometimes put a little in the bank.

I worked at the post office about one and a half years. Then as I was married, my husband Dick and I moved to Columbus, Ohio, and then to Louisville, Kentucky for two and a half years. This was wartime and Dick worked in an airplane plant, as he was classified in 4F because of a perforated eardrum, and didn't qualify for military service. We enjoyed living there and made some good friends, but we were more than ready to move back to Ohio to be near family and old friends, and to await the birth of our first child after the war had ended.

Now back to some childhood memories. Dad had a couple hives of bees and we would sometimes get a little too close and get stung, so Mom would mix up some soda paste and put it on the burning and itching welt. Dad made a protective covering for his face and neck, by attaching some netting to one of his old felt hats. This kept him from being stung, as he took some honey from the hives. I can almost see him now. So many memories are stored in my brain. How wonderful!

Dad tried many ways to provide little extras for the family. He raised two or three hogs one year, and I remember Mom and I staying inside the house when butchering day arrived. A local butcher came down to help Dad with this rather frightening and upsetting job, at least if felt that way to me, but it provided us with pork for many a month.

Mom always canned many things and had lots of hard work, with cooking, sewing, and doing mounds of laundry. For years she washed clothes in an old washtub with a scrub board, and what a help it was, when Dad bought a nice Maytag, gasoline powered washing machine. You could hear it all over the neighborhood in summer, because Mom would do the washing on the back porch. In later years an electric motor was attached in place of the old gasoline one and Mom used if for many years, until she finally got an automatic washer and dryer. Sure wish something like that had been available when she had such a large family.

I can always find a story to tell about my mom. We had a neighbor who lived around the corner from us and her family owned a Model T Ford. One late summer day, she loaded it full of her children, Mom and some of our family, and we went for a country ride. They could see corn ripening in the fields and decided it would taste mighty good for our evening meal, so she and Mom got out and picked some for our families. I can't remember if they paid the farmer, but I'm sure he wouldn't have cared, because there was row after row of field corn waving in the breeze.

One Fall that same neighbor and Mom decided to make apple butter, with apples from the big old tree in our back yard. It took lots of peeling and cutting, but they would joke and have fun at the job. A huge iron kettle over an open fire in the yard, and stirring with the big long wooden paddle, would keep them busy most of the day. After it was cooked down and nice and brown, they poured it into earthenware jars and sealed them up for a tasty winter treat. A job well done, and I'm sure they were more than ready to hop into bed that night.

Halloween time has just passed and all the young ones, most dressed in elaborate costumes, were going from house to house and getting candy treats. Some would have a pillowcase full!

Things were different when I was small. No fancy costumes, just anything we could find from family clothes. Hobo was a pretty easy one to put together and lots of us would dress that way. Kids now probably hardly know anything about hobos. They were homeless men who would jump from a freight train as it slowed down going through Kingston, and some of them used to stop at our house asking for a meal. Mom would fix them something and they would eat on the porch before going on.

We never had what we called trick or treat night, but would go to neighbors and have them try to guess who we were. As a teenager, we would soap windows, throw corn, and sometimes cabbage heads, or anything from a garden onto porches around town, and then run as fast as we could. Teenage boys always managed to knock over a few outhouses and stay one step ahead of the village marshal. I can't remember anyone going to jail. Nowadays, I'm sure it would not be taken lightly. It just seemed to be an accepted part of Halloween then. Sure wasn't very nice, but we thought it was fun.

Old Goth Hall on Oak Street, used to be the scene for many evenings of entertainment. It was at one time used for a skating rink, round and square dances, and medicine shows, where they put on acts, sold their patent medicines, and boxes of candy with a prize inside. As a kid, I had fun there. Also boxing matches were held and probably many other things. It was at one time a place for making soda pop, called the Grapette Company, and it was a success for a good many years.

Now that I think back, Kingston was livelier then, than it is now, but we sometimes thought it was a little dull. During the school year, we kept pretty busy with Basketball games, school plays, class parties, and an occasional dance.

A banquet would be held each spring honoring the ball players, and pea patties would always be on the menu. For those who never heard of them, it was a tiny individual piecrust with creamed peas inside. They weren't bad, if you liked peas.

Later in the year, we had the Junior-Senior Prom, where the pretty formals on the girls and suits on the boys, made us feel pretty snazzy. Our family didn't have much money then, so I ordered a long pink taffeta dress from the famous Sears Roebuck Catalog for five bucks. It was really pretty too! I imagine some of the other girls used that old catalog, though they were probably ashamed to admit it. In earlier years those Catalogs met their demise in the old outhouse.

Another happy memory of school days comes to mind. My old friends, Phyllis, Marvene, Jean and I were basketball cheerleaders. Phyllis and I had the loud mouths for the job, and all of us together had a few fancy moves so we would soon have some cheering fans. The school colors were red and blue, and our uniforms of bright red skirts, white sweaters, and blue shirts, were pleasing to the eye. We always got into the games free, which was a big plus, and I guess we felt kind of important too.

Then many years before that, when I was in the third or fourth grade, I was required to learn many of the states and their capitals. I would practice them out loud, in the evenings at home. Sister, Margaret, was just a little tyke about three years old, and she would listen to me. It wasn't long before she knew them as well as I did. Naturally I was proud of her, and I took her to school for a visit so she could recite them for the teachers and my classmates. They thought she was really smart and pretty cute too. I think I could almost write a book about my school days.

Not everyone had a car in those days, so the streets were often used as a playground for many. A side street for softball games, of course, roller skating, toy wagons, and a carnival was held right up town on Main Street for many years.

I remember one year at Christmas time a big evergreen tree was set up in the intersection up town, and the few cars had to drive around. It created much excitement, as Santa would be there in his bright red suit, and pass out candy treats to each little girl and boy. I was very small then, but this is one of my earliest childhood memories.

Then last but not least, every Christmas time, an old nodding Santa Claus proudly stood in the window of the Yaple and Hassenpflu Store on the corner, and it was a delight to many all through the years.

I know I loved the little town of Kingston then, and I still do. Ah, childhood and memories, how dear you are!

This is Main Street in Kingston, 2007

~ Days Gone By (2004) ~

I have always heard that as you grow older you think more of the past. It's happening to me now that I have reached eighty. I felt the desire to pass some of the memories of my life as I remember them to the younger generation.

It was a good time to live back in the late 1920s, 30s, and early 40s. Life was at a much slower pace back then. Everyone was poor, but as children we didn't really know it. Ah, the innocence of youth!

Our future years are influenced by the many things of our past so I hope you enjoy reading about the times I shared with my family.

Our grandma, dad's mother, and our step-grandpa lived with our family for a time. They had come to Ohio after living in Georgia and Florida for quite a few years. They later rented a little house not too far from ours. Grandpa did odd jobs, was church janitor, and for a time was Marshal of our little Kingston Village. We sure had a houseful when they lived with us. With five girls, a couple of dogs, and a cat or two, we were quite a family. Don't quite know where we all slept. I remember grandma made good graham cracker pudding. A dessert with bananas and her own special vanilla sauce. Just give us something sweet and we were happy.

Our dogs were part German Shepherd. Trixie was the mommy. Dad found her over on the railroad and brought her home. She was expecting puppies and later gave birth to five balls of fur. We gave them all away but one male. We named him "Wimpy," but he was always called "Pup." He used to follow me to school and often came in the open door of the old schoolhouse and would come up the stairs to my room. Sometimes Mr. Ellis, my teacher, would let him stay awhile and lie down by my desk. Trixie developed a growth and it became an open sore so she had to be put to sleep after we had her for a few years. Old Pup lived to be at least twelve and put many a scare into the town cats during his roamings.

Dad used to buy us lots of fireworks for the 4th of July. He would set off the most dangerous ones and enjoyed doing it for he never had things like that as a child. Still is a wonder we didn't get hurt setting off those firecrackers. When we had Trixie, she was afraid of the loud noise, so she would take off for the country, but she always returned. Lots of times we went to Chillicothe Park for the fireworks and carnival. July 4th was a happy holiday.

My old friend Marvene lived just around the corner from us. The first time I remember seeing her she was on her porch playing with a little green piano. I asked her to come to my house sometime and bring it with her. Through the years we spent lots of time together, staying all night with each other, making fudge and just hanging out. Her dad would take us to movies, swimming, and sometimes I would go to their family reunions. We also walked to and from school together and remained friends into our old age.

When we lived on Ford Street our house had a bathtub but only an outside toilet. There was a hot water heater but we didn't always have it lit, only special times. The tank had to be filled by a valve we turned at our kitchen pump. Most people didn't have indoor plumbing. The old outhouse had to be periodically cleaned and the toilet cleaners, they were called "honey dippers" would come late in the night so the smell wouldn't be noticed too much by us or our neighbors. The old outhouse wasn't too pleasant, but very necessary.

My sister Pauline tells me the story of how she and a friend got in our dad's Model A Ford which was parked in front of our house, and she drove it several blocks around town. She didn't really know how to drive either. She parked it in a different direction when she got home and our dad never found out she drove it. He never said a word. I didn't think Pauline had that much nerve.

I just had to add this about Pauline. Teresa, her daughter, recently told me that Pauline liked to sew some of her own clothes while she was still living at home with mom and dad. One time she pinned a pattern for a dress on material she had placed on the bed. As she was cutting it out she not only cut the fabric, but through the bed quilt as well. Teresa wasn't sure if she was at home at the time or visiting an aunt. Talk about life's embarrassing moments, that was one!

One time when Edna was about ten or eleven she found a can or bottle of dry cleaning fluid. She was lying on the old leather davenport and I guess she liked the smell so she got kinda high. Dad raised the roof! Of course it was mom's fault he said.

Mom used to bake the best sugar cookies. She was a good cook and we had plenty to eat during the depression years. We were very fortunate as dad always had a good job as Section Foreman on the C & O Railroad. We always called it dad's railroad when we took a ride and drove on the overpass.

I remember mom smoked a little and she would roll her own from tins of Prince Albert and Velvet tobacco. She never taught us girls how to cook and dad always said we would never learn. Not to be bragging but after we were all married we became pretty good cooks. Experience is a great teacher.

An old couple, Mr. and Mrs. Hannawalt, lived next door to us on Ford Street. He was blind and needed lots of care. Their older son, when he was a man, lived with them for a time. Mom and dad's bedroom window and their kitchen window were not too far apart and I remember mom told the story of seeing Will, the son, as naked as a jaybird and washing his clothes on the washboard in an old galvanized tub. He was just scrubbing away! That was quite a sight!

I know when I was a small child and we lived in Kentucky my older sister Ginny was so dear to me. She helped to take care of me and always made me feel very special. I fell and knocked one of my front teeth out while she was away one time and I remember when she came home I ran to her crying and she picked me up to console me. I know I loved her very much.

Sister Margaret was the baby of the family and she had a head full of beautiful blonde curls. Dad used to call her "Old Hossfly." I remember hearing the story that when Margaret was a little girl she went to the grocery store with mom. Mom had told her she needed bread, cereal, meat and so forth. Well, mom gave the order to the grocer, Mr. Yaple, and Margaret said, "Mom, you forgot the so forth." I guess she thought that was something we really needed.

Then one summer day Margaret and her friend Betty were outside playing. Mom could hear them running up on the back porch but thought nothing of it. It was later discovered that they were eating chocolate Ex-Lax squares that had been put in our back porch icebox. I know that they each ate enough that the path to the outhouse was used a lot that day. Seems there was never a dull moment when we were growing up.

Coming home from school one day I was surprised to see the village fire truck there. Smoke was pouring from the roof of our house and the firemen were up there with the big hose trying to put it out. Not too much damage, but that was scary! I guess a faulty fireplace caused the fire to start. I don't know if we stayed there that night. This was our house on Pickaway Street and it still stands today.

Also remember a very bad storm that blew most of the window panes out of our house. Must have been straight line winds. We had coal oil lamps so it was a wonder we didn't have a fire. No one was hurt, but I know we didn't stay there that night. Dad and Uncle Ayrus boarded up the windows and we went down to stay with Aunt Lizzie, mom's sister. That was the little house we first lived in when we moved from Kentucky. We didn't live there too long after that.

Mom raised chickens when we lived on Ford Street and at Cedar Grove for eggs and meat. Mom would never kill one so dad had to do the job and she would never watch. They always tasted so good, fried with her good brown gravy. I could eat some right now. Chicken today just doesn't have that good taste.

We usually had good Christmases and the tree stood in the best room of the house. It was not always heated so it was pretty cold in there and the tree stayed fresh and green. What stands out most in my mind were the colorful handkerchiefs spread on the branches and the bags of candy, oranges, and bananas under the tree. Of course, we got dolls and other things too. I can still remember the smell of pine as we entered the room. These things are forever imprinted on my mind.

Sometimes Uncle Joe and Aunt Edna would come to visit grandma, grandpa, and our family. She was Dad's sister and they lived in Indiana. They had no children and Uncle Joe always made over us. I remember him taking us to Mead Park Swimming Pool, and they always brought boxes of candy, usually chocolate-covered cherries. Of course we liked for them to visit.

One year Edna my sister went home with Aunt Edna and Uncle Joe. A few weeks later Mom, Margaret, and I went out on the train and stayed for a week. Uncle Joe took us to Lake Erie for a swim while we were there. Edna and all of us came home on the train after our visit. I was probably about thirteen so this was quite an experience as I had never been that far from home before.

We used to have lots of fun when we lived on Ford Street. There were lots and lots of kids in our neighborhood. We played "Go Sheepie Go," "Hide-and-Seek," softball, and sometimes got together and told ghost stories. Sled writing in the winter was always fun too. Later, we walked up town when old enough, and hung out at the restaurant with friends.

We used to go to some old swimming holes sometimes. They were much cleaner then but still dangerous. On one such occasion some older boys pulled an inner tube away from Bob and me, leaving us in water over our heads. Someone had to get us out because we were not good swimmers at that time. That was rather frightening.

Mom used to be quite a practical joker. She and her sisters had a laughing good time when they got together after they were married and had families of their own. One time when she was packing her suitcase after a visit with my aunt Hazel, she put one of Aunt Hazel's dresses in her suitcase, fastened the lid, and made sure part of the dress was hanging out. She pretended that she really wanted the dress and they had a good laugh over that episode. They told us the story many times over the years.

Then one year at Easter, Edna carefully made a nest of grass and put it in the corner waiting for a visit from the Easter Bunny. Mom could not resist the temptation so she went out in the yard and found a nice dried up dog dropping and put it in the nest. Edna was really hurt and never let mom forget it all through the years.

Edna and I finally saved up enough money in our school bank accounts for a nice balloon tire bicycle. Dad bought it in Chillicothe and I'm pretty sure it was $29.95. It was a pretty blue-and-white, with shiny fenders. We brought it into the house and could hardly sleep. We just kept looking at it and anxious for the rides the next morning. We were so proud. We lived on Ford Street then.

We moved from that house, I think about 1939, and went to live at the house in the field on the east side of Kingston. It was pretty shabby inside with wallpaper hanging from the ceiling and just needing lots of repairs. They were soon taken care of and we all loved that old place. It was red brick with a yard full of cedar and shade trees, so the name, "Cedar Grove."

It had a country look with horses and cows grazing in the field outside our yard. While living there we all walked on the path through the field on our many trips to town and school. Sometimes we came home in the dark of night and had a fear of falling over a sleeping cow, a horse running us down, or stepping in "you know what." Those were the days!

I still think of mom when I smell Petunias. She had a window box full of them at the Cedar Grove house, and when we had the window open we could smell them as we ate our meal at the kitchen table. I can also picture dad as he used his hand plow in his big vegetable garden. These things you don't easily forget.

In later years Cedar Grove was divided into lots and houses were built. The trees, horses, and cows are all gone now, but the old house still stands as a reminder of the days gone by.

Cedar Grove as it appeared when the author was growing up

Another image of Cedar Grove

~ **My Old School Days (1991)** ~

How well I remember that old school bell of long ago - ringing out to tell us it would soon be time to go.

We usually listened eagerly for that first bell, for then we could leave home to join our friends on the playground, or in the classroom on rainy days. School was the highlight of our social life.

We didn't have TVs, VCRs, or all those modern means of entertainment. We had to make up our own games. How well I remember roller skating down the long concrete sidewalks from the schoolhouse to the street. How wonderful were all the picnics and the programs we had on the last day of school each year!

Everything moved at a slower pace back then. "Humpty Dumpty Sat on a Wall," "Little Miss Muffit Sat on a Tuffet," "Little Jack Horner Sat in a Corner." Everybody seemed to be sitting. In later years, it was "Run Spot Run." I must ask my daughter, a first grade teacher, about the 80s and 90s. They are probably in space ships by now.

At lunch time - home we'd go, and for those of us who lived across town from the schoolhouse, we worked up a pretty good appetite for the lunch our mothers were preparing for us at home. Most mothers were full-time homemakers in those days.

Families were larger, and rooms were shared, usually two and sometimes three, to a bed. Not much privacy then! Most of us had a little house out the back. City water was a thing of the future, and old well pumps graced most back yards, usually with an apple tree close by, where we used to climb and sit high, dreaming on a summer day.

As I look back at each school year, one little thing stands out. Mary Ford was my first grade teacher, and I still see her with the pointer under each word as we slowly learned to read. A large book stood on a stand in the front of the room. I can see her turning over the big, big pages even now. They seemed so large to a little six-year old.

If I remember right, Mrs. May was my second grade teacher. Can't remember much about her, except she made me stay after school one day. Then I remember when I was older and she died - all the school kids marched to her house to view the body. Maybe these aren't the best of memories.

Then, third, and fourth, grade, Miss Thomas taught me. I know she was a wonderful teacher, but can't recall much of that. But I can envision her writing in our bank books on "bank day" because our dad usually gave each of us girls 25 cents to deposit. Sometimes I wonder how he did that. These were depression days, but he had a steady job as section foreman on the C&O Railroad. One year he was very sick and off work, so we had a pretty hard time then.

Sometime during our grade school years, my sister Edna and I saved enough money to buy a nice balloon-tire bicycle. I remember staying awake most of the night admiring it.

In fourth grade I had a boyfriend named Bob, and he was passing some paper all the way across the room to me, which caught the attention of Miss Thomas. She said something about it in front of the whole class - was I embarrassed!

In the fifth grade, I had Miss Ada for a teacher, but have few memories of that year.

Then, sixth year - Mr. Ellis was my first male teacher. I liked him very much and was often told I was teacher's pet. I was a hard worker that year. I often made up questions to help me study for history and geography tests and Mr. Ellis would sometimes have me ask them to the class. Another fond memory - I had an old part German Shepherd dog named "Pup," who used to follow me to school. He made many appearances in our school room, Mr. Ellis often letting him lie down by my desk. This is one of my most memorable years.

Childhood days are left behind as I went into seventh and eighth grades. No more recess! Changing class for each subject was an exciting thing for a while. At least it was exercise. Boys are now beginning to have a new importance in my life. Studying for some subjects which I didn't like were shoved into the background. At the end of eighth grade, I had my eyes on a certain boy, Dick, who later became my husband.

As a freshman and sophomore, I played some basketball, but was too short to be much good, although I was a scrapper. I spent a lot of time on the floor. Algebra was a favorite subject that year. Another highlight, I was chosen queen of the Halloween carnival, and my boyfriend, Dick, was king. That's the only time I have been royalty. Also, I played the lead role in an operetta called, "Chonita," and you guessed it, the leading male role, was played by my boyfriend. Must have been fate.

During my junior year, I became a cheerleader. I can see the blue and red satin outfit yet. Hot stuff, huh? The senior year outfit was more modern, I guess. Red short, short, skirt, white sweater, brown and white saddle shoes and knee-socks. Those were fun times, except when we lost some crucial basketball games with our big rival, Centralia.

My senior and final year was more of the same. Still not much studying done except for bookkeeping and things I liked. Sorry Mr. Ellis, history took too much time.

Graduation pictures were taken - such a big thing - had the whole day to travel to Columbus - no school - good. I always thought I had an ugly smile, so my picture was sober as a judge. The year was full - plays, concerts, cheerleading, ball games, banquets, and Boys!! Remembering classes again. I took public speaking, which was a favorite. Had plays and learned many poems. The teacher was a "gem" - Miss Elliott. She wore her hair pulled back in a knot - a very attractive lady with warm brown eyes and a ready smile.

Graduation night finally came. There were lots of tears. School years to be left behind, and life was to be pursued at a more serious level. At 17, I wasn't quite ready for that.

Looking back, there were many teachers that stand out. Mr. Miraben, basketball coach, Miss Hampton, Mr. Uhl, Mr. Bernard, and Mr. Sutherland, and Mr. Holmes who were superintendents. I can see the faces of many others in my mind, and remember some things that stand out about them.

Happy times and unhappy times, spats with boyfriends and girlfriends, sometimes worrying about tests (should have studied more), a big ball game - being selected cheerleader, wanting to be popular - all a part of school days and growing up.

Time so swiftly passes and now I'm approaching old age - some would say I am already in it. Before too many years, I'll be graduating from the "school of life." Hope I am more prepared for that than I was for my high school graduation.

~ The Lonesome Puppy (2009) ~

Blackie liked his big doghouse in the shady backyard. The days were warm and sunny, and sometimes a little girl would play with him. His bowl was filled with cold water and his food was brought each day. He was a happy little puppy.

Then the rains began to fall and Blackie's yard was covered in mud. His feet would get all dirty and no little girl came to play. He felt so alone.

The days grew colder and Blackie huddled in his big doghouse. Oh, how he waited for the warm sunshine.

Christmas eve came and again Blackie shivered in the cold. Then a glorious thing happened. He felt a great warmth and happiness in his heart, for the back door of the house opened, and a friendly little voice called out. "Here Blackie, come inside, you'll be really cozy and warm." He joyfully ran into the open door, and two arms reached for him. The miracle of Christmas had come to a lonesome little puppy.

~ Thinking Back ~

When Jonathan and David were born in 1978 I was so thrilled but also a little afraid. It was such an awesome task. Sometimes I wonder how Jeanne lived through it. Don't believe I could have stood up to it as well even though I helped her as much as I could for the first few months. Being a Mother isn't easy. I think I always made a big deal of it and didn't relax the way I should. It is such a wonderful experience if you just relax.

I can look out the window now sometimes and remember how Jeanne used to come flying down with the boys in the baby buggy for their morning visit.

Also remember how when they were a little older they played "garbage man" and would dump everything they could find in the middle of the family room floor at my house including junk from the waste basket. What a mess!

Thinking back when Dick put the partitions in the basement of the parsonage. Barry was the minister of the Methodist Church here in Kingston. The boys were about two years old and they went around with hammer and nails wanting to be carpenters.

They had swings in the basement and they wanted to swing every time their Grandpa and I went up to visit. Of course they wanted to go so high that they could touch the ceiling with their feet. Scared me! Not them though.

Oh the many years of playing store. I always had to buy my own canned goods etc. I think every can and box came out of my cupboards.

Spent many hours sewing little stuffed animals, mainly bears and making clothes for them. The boys always found names that seemed to suit them.

Then all the stories I made up. They always wanted Grandma to tell a story. After so many years of stories my old brain could hardly make up another one. Of course they usually helped me along the way and they got pretty funny.

Also would take walks when they came down and would usually have most of the neighborhood kids along and "old Blackie" my cat following close behind. We sometimes ended up at the waterworks and they would dip their hands in the water and then chase after me so they could wipe their hands on my clothes.

As they got older we would play baseball with me as chief pitcher. Also spent time rolling down the waterworks hill and watching the trains and waving to the engineer. They would sometimes blow the whistle which thrilled all the kids. Played hide and seek too. You can't be a child without that.

I can see them yet when they were small. I would go up to visit and when they would spy me they'd yell "Grandma" and their eyes would light up just like I was the most wonderful person in the whole world. Sure made me feel special.

Then the many telephone calls I had always wanting to come down or wanting me to order something from their "Bay Biddle Restaurant." I ordered many things but don't remember any deliveries. What imaginations they have always had.

At Christmas time, probably when they were about three years old, we would make sugar cookies. Each of them with one of my aprons on and with a rolling pin they would start. One on a chair at the kitchen cupboards and the other at the island counter. After much rolling and throwing flour around, they would cut them in different shapes. The gingerbread boy was the favorite. After they were baked they spread icing of different colors on each one. The kitchen sure needed a thorough cleaning when they were done. We all had lots of fun with this Christmas tradition.

They also loved to go upstairs and jump up and down on my old bed and had great fun working on an old sewing machine of mine. They removed every screw and all the parts they could and then they pounded it to death. The trash man finally got that but they amused themselves for quite a few visits.

On lots of visits the toy dump trucks would be brought out and they would load them with their stuffed bears and push them all through the house just as fast as possible. What fun!

Grandpa started giving them $10.00 a month allowance when they were real small. They seemed to think that it was pay because they'd say "Have you paid us for this month yet, Grandpa?"

They also had to have snacks when they came and orange juice, cookies, and milk shakes were favorite things. Always liked to take baths in my bathtub too. We would put in lots of bubbles and a tub-full of toys to play with. The bathroom later became a great reading room. They were always fond of reading and they sure should have been because we all read to them before they could walk or talk.

At 11 years of age they would go to the Nursing Home to visit the people there. On Saturday afternoons we'd play bingo and while I called the numbers they would help the players find the numbers on their cards. We would usually give candy, cookies, and gum as prizes. They especially liked talking to Dorsey. Everyone enjoyed seeing them. They were good boys to take time to visit those old people. Sometimes the place smelled kinda bad but we tried to ignore it. Sure wish they'd make things more pleasant for those poor people. I told Jonathan to not let me go there. If I get too bad just shoot me. It's a sad thing to happen to anyone.

Grandsons David and Jonathan, age 2 ½, cleaning up after eating icing (most of it made it on their faces)

Section Two: Poems

~ Christmas Long Ago (2004) ~

When I think of Christmas and childhood
All the years so long ago,
Sometimes days would be warm and pleasant,
Then along would come the deep snow.

A proud Christmas tree would beckon from our front room,
Which was colder than the rest,
But a potbellied stove aglow with warmth,
Made it feel the very best.

The smell of pine from the tall old tree,
All decked out with balls and garlands of red,
Made it so hard on Christmas Eve,
To climb our long stairs up to bed.

Then snuggled down in a featherbed,
I just knew Santa was over our house.
I'd look out the window, then jump back into bed,
And try to be quiet as a mouse.

I could picture his reindeer with his sleigh full of toys,
Especially a doll for me!
Then the next thing I knew, morning had come,
So I jumped out of bed with glee.

Now light as air I raced down the stairs
And into that glorious room.

All of my sisters, the dogs, oh the havoc!
Now Mom and Dad would enter real soon.

The branches were adorned with hankies,
Which Santa had placed on the tree.
Toys, oranges, and candy in bags,
Awaited my sisters and me.

Oh the joy of Christmas so long ago
Will always have a place in my heart,
For now, my Mom, my Dad and my sisters,
Have for many long years been apart.

~ A Childhood Doll (1991) ~

A precious little friend,
Has come to live with me.
Never frowning, always smiling,
As far as I can see.

Her hair is brightest yellow,
and her eyes are azure blue,
She wears a frilly little dress,
And her shoes are shiny and new.

I tell her that I love her,
But those words she cannot say,
You see her body's filled with stuffing,
And her head is made of clay.

Even though she cannot tell me,
I know she is my friend,
She whispers to me everyday,
In our game of "let's pretend."

~ Evening Twilight (2001) ~

Walking in the evening twilight,
On streets still wet with rain,
With thoughts and cares of daily life,
Still passing through my brain.

Suddenly the chirps of robins,
On lawns all over town,
Awoke me to the beauties,
That upon the earth abound.

Trees in all their majesty,
Branches raised toward the darkening sky –
Some so old and gnarled,
Their time soon come to die.

I always feel a sadness,
When the buzz of a saw is heard,
To know a tree is gone forever,
No longer shelter for a little bird.

But God in all his glory,
With sunshine and the rain,
Will cause a seed still dormant,
To come to life again.

~ Stormy Times ~

A loud boom of thunder breaks the silence of the air.
Our prayer for rain is answered, from a sky no longer fair

Mothballs of hail bounce all along the ground.
The rain upon the rooftop brings such a joyful sound.

The trees rock back and forth, dancing to and fro.
The birds dart from their branches, all singing as they go.

We see our Lord's directing hand of his orchestra up on high.
It shows his great love for us, and we need never wonder why.

Joyful, joyful, is the splendor of the skies.
Oh Lord, we adore Thee, with a love that never dies.

~ **In Times of Storm** ~

On a hot July night in 1998
When storm clouds start to form,
my anxious eyes search the skies.
Soon flashes of light pierce the darkness,
and claps of thunder break the silence.
Birds scurry for a hiding place as the tree branches start to sway,
and the rain dances on the roof.
All God's way of cooling and watering the earth.

Why do I worry? He will be in control.

Afterwards a calmness prevails and once more,
we have been spared a violent storm.

My old sump pump in the basement didn't growl at all,
and all is at peace.
Thank you, God.

~ Night Time (June 2007) ~

Deep in the night the wind was still,
The trees their branches clothed in leaves,
So quiet as though resting,
No chirps of birds could be heard

A blanket of clouds covered the stars,
Their light faintly dimmed.
The grass formed a place of rest for each little bug,
All was peaceful.

Somewhere the call of an owl broke the silence
But no one roused from their sleep.
On a nearby farm a cow quietly munched some grass,
Before lying down on a bed moist from the dew.

A corn field close by grew tall, with no one watching
Harvest time was growing near
Each day provides the bounty of God's goodness,
That even man so small, will feel his love

Now in the stillness of the night may we find rest and peace
Freedom from our daily chores, and our souls
In the hands of God.
Sleep well, my friends, sleep well.

~ Thank You Prayer (July 1999) ~

Thank you God for sunshine,
And for each little breeze,
that brings to us a greeting,
From the leaves on all the trees.

Thank you God for clouds,
Where angels dwell at night,
Keeping watch while we are sleeping,
Until morning brings us light...

Thank you God for birds,
and squirrels and rabbits too,
But most of all for your presence,
In everything we do.

~ A Country Visit (June 2001) ~

Skies were bright blue,
with mottled clouds of white.
Brilliant yellow sunshine,
was casting rays of light.

A magnificent red barn,
So very proudly stood,
Where once a gentle cow,
May have quietly chewed her cud.

Near the still waters of the majestic pond,
A family of Canada geese made their home.
A little white duck came to join them,
Who for days had lived all alone.

Now some contented cats were waiting,
to greet us at the door,
The pungent smell of herbs and flowers,
who could have asked for more?

The peaceful quiet of a country scene,
How calming to the heart,
Thank you God for giving to us,
A day so set apart.

~ My Cat (May 1998) ~

Yellow and fuzzy,
Sweet and fat,
These words will tell you,
About my cat.

Sleeps a lot,
And bird watches too,
Eats like a pig,
And looks like a moo.

Sometimes a little mean,
But loving she can be.
Her purrs are long and loud,
And her happiness you can see.

I think she must love me,
But doesn't often show it,
But all the contentment she gives to me,
Helps me through each moment.

~ My Back Porch ~

Rocking on my back porch,
On pleasant summer days,
Brings lots of joy into my heart,
In so very many ways.

The frisky little rabbits,
Give chase so very fast,
It must be lots and lots of fun,
For it seems to last and last.

Now the squirrels vie for my attention,
As they chase each other up and down the trees,
The flowers in their brilliant colors,
So inviting to the hungry bees.

The birds are singing happily,
As they come to search for food,
Then busily flying to their nest,
As they feed their waiting brood.

How I love the things of nature,
So interesting it can be,
If only we will take the time,
These magical joys to see

~ Dandelions (April 2005) ~

Dandelions put on their hats of yellow,
To greet the days of spring.
In the fields, the yards, and hillsides
A most glorious sight they bring.

In the town's old schoolyard,
I saw them dancing in grasses of green,
Where our children on the playground,
So seldom now are seen.

Then at times some little ones
Will come to play a game of ball,
Perhaps picking some of the yellow posies,
Before the shadows fall.

With a smile they hand them to their mothers,
As a gift to show their love,
We now see why God made dandelions,
They're most likely from heaven above.

Now all too soon the hats of yellow,
Become gray and flit away,
But for a time their brilliant color,
Brought some love and beauty to the day.

~ The Old Elm Tree (April 2005) ~

Dedicated to my children Ricky and Jeanne, their cousins, and my grandsons, David and
Jonathan

The old elm tree came down today,
I think the birds and squirrels all cried.
It proudly shaded our backyard,
'Twas long our joy and pride.

Beneath its shady branches,
Our children used to play.
It saw days of picnics and volleyball,
While keeping the sun at bay.

The owls, squirrels, and birds,
In its holes made nests.
Its branches provided a playground,
And a place for long night's rests.

But now, many of its branches,
Are broken down and weak.
The storms and high winds of life,
Have caused its limbs to moan and creak.

You see its trunk is rather wrinkled,

As ages does to a man.

We now let it go regretfully,

Remembering, when children beneath it ran.

The spring has come to clothe it all in green once more,

I know I'll miss its friendly shade,

But still, the memories of its glory

In my heart will never fade.

~ **Morning Prayer (2002)** ~

Sitting in my chair each morning,
The Lord is always near to me,
As I seek His daily guidance,
He opens my eyes to see.

I thank him for my safety
All throughout the night.
Especially when I get restful sleep,
And awake to sunlight bright.

I thank Him for my family,
That He may bless each one.
That He'll give them safety and guidance,
Until the day is done.

I pray He'll touch the sick
And put peace deep within.
Their pain He'll help to bear,
And He'll release them from their sin.

I thank Him for freedom,
To worship Him each day.
I give Him thanks for life and health.
My path, he'll show the way.

~ My Old Elm Tree (2002) ~

In my back yard, a tall old elm tree,
So very proudly stands,
All clothed in green this time of year,
Not fashioned by human hands.

Her branches spread out far and wide,
Her shade she gives to all.
The birds nest in her branches;
There the squirrels hoard nuts for fall.

Once under her bright canopy of leaves,
Little children used to run and play.
Their voices lifting among the branches,
Such joyful sounds each day.

But now those little children,
Into adults have grown.
That lonely tree stands silent,
Sometimes, I think I hear it moan.

Does it miss the sounds of childhood?
I do, I can't deny,
But the memories of yesterday,
Bring smiles, sometimes tears, of days gone by.

~ Saturday Shopping (August 2000) ~

A Saturday of shopping
Is the highlight of my week.
Up and down each aisle of groceries,
For something new I seek.

From cereal to cat food,
Ice cream and fruits too.
I pause to read some labels,
To see what things will do.

Then a bright red bottle,
Really caught my eye.
Just a little in your water,
would give wrinkles a good-bye.

I could hardly wait for home,
So this product I could try.
So hurried there and filled my tub,
And didn't blink an eye.

Now in sudsy water,
Clear up to my chin,
It wouldn't be too long,
until this wrinkle battle, I would win.

When the time was up,

For it to do its work,

I grabbed my towel, looked in the mirror,

Boy was I a jerk!

That product sure didn't work,

I could plainly see.

I'd better read that label --

For your clothes instead of me.

Now all dressed up and ready to go,

But with water still in the tub

I jumped in and splashed about

To give them a little rub.

Now my clothes came out as good as new,

But my skin was still a mess,

The character still showing there --

Will keep that bottle for my clothes, I guess

~ Autumn (October 1, 1999) ~

Diamonds of dust glowing on the window,
When the sun shines through.
There's beauty all around us,
As each day, the grass is kissed by dew.

Trees dressed in all their glory,
With garbs of red, yellow, and green.
Man's paint brush could never capture,
What human eye has seen.

Only God can create the beauty,
Because of love for man,
Such radiance and majesty,
Throughout this glorious land.

So take the time to thank Him,
For the blessings that we share.
Only with a "thank you"
Will he know how much we care.

~ The Old Hall (February 2002) ~

How well I remember the old medicine shows
That took place in the old Goth Hall.
In between the acts on the stage
They would peddle their wares to all.

"Get your tonic here."
One big bottle for fifty cents!
Come on ladies, a cure for you,
and even you manly gents.

From all your aches and pains,
To even bouts of depression,
This bottle would surely take care
Of most any situation.

But being a child, the acts on the stage,
Always made me clap with glee.
I had no use for that stuff in the bottle,
The candy they sold was a delight to me.

A prize sometimes would be in the box
Along with many a candy kiss.
You see, the joys of my happy childhood,
Are filled with memories, just like this.

~ That Old Tonic of Days Gone By (February 2002) ~

Are you tired, run down, and listless?
Has your life lost its zing?
Just one big bottle of our tonic,
Will make you want to sing.

Full of vitamins and minerals,
And yet it's tasty too.
You'll wonder why just yesterday,
You felt so very blue.

So just for fifty cents a bottle,
That's all you have to pay.
Your life will get much better,
With every passing day.

~ School Days (2002) ~

The part of our lives we spent in school,
Is in our memories yet.
We all must have a story to tell,
On that, I'll surely bet.

For some that big old school bell
Would ring out loud and clear.
We'd gather up our books and leave our homes,
To meet our friends so dear.

We must not forget our teachers,
Who tried to fill our brains with learnin'
While we did the best we could sometimes,
For the outside, we all were yearnin'.

Now that old back-house was very near,
So when nature made its call,
Our hands would raise high in the air,
Then we'd rush on down the hall.

At recess time we'd hurry out,
To begin our time of play,
Down the slide, jumping rope, and playing ball,
could be part of that fun day.

I'm sure you younger grads,
Have your fond memories too,
Times were somewhat different then,
In things you could say and do.

I remember how the band would play,
And march up and down each street.
How proud we were and happy too,
As we watched those white clad feet.

Now those days have left us,
But deep inside each heart,
The memories are forever with us,
So with them, we'll never part.

~ **Birds (2001)** ~

I'm sure God loves each little bird,
He gave them wings to fly.
Soaring close to heaven,
in a sun filled sky.

So close he might reach out His hand
To stroke their feathered wings,
Just to show his love for them,
And give them joy to sing.

Some he dressed in coats of red,
And others are brightest blue.
But precious in His Godly eyes
Are those of every hue.

~ Summer Rain (2001) ~

A gentle rain is a gift from God,
After a hot and muggy day,
Making little puddles
Where children like to play.

Each little flower lifts up its colorful head,
Trees stretch out their branches,
Nudging sleeping birds
From their cozy beds.

A new day is beginning
With the earth awash anew,
Garden plants are growing,
And weeds are sprouting too.

Corn in fields so green and tall,
Will reap a Fall reward.
Mother Nature's been good to us,
So give thanks unto the Lord.

~ Memories of Edna (February 2003) ~

My sister Edna and I
Through the years shared many things.
The same room, the same bed,
And all that childhood brings.

Some days I'm sure we weren't friends,
Like all kids, we sometimes had a spat.
But I know we really loved each other
In spite of all of that.

Lots of our friends were the same,
As our ages were not far apart.
The memories of the fun we had,
Come from deep inside the heart.

We were so happy the time Mom and Dad
Drove the old Ford to town,
They bought us a shiny new bike
And that night we could hardly lie down.

It caused a few fights sometimes
Of who would ride it off to school.
We could get there in a jiffy,
And to our classmates look so cool.

After we were married,
We gathered with friends for lunch.
We had good food and lots of gab,
We were a lively bunch.

One time when friends sat around my table,
Edna knocked upon my door,
Garbed in a grotesque outfit,
I almost fell on the floor.

Bright rouge upon her cheeks,
No smile upon her face,
I thought she'd lost her marbles,
Surely a basket case.

Then a big grin came upon her face,
So I felt it safe to let her in.
She was the life of the party that day
And I was glad she was my kin.

That's just a good example
Of the sense of humor that was there,
I'll remember it always
And for her I'll always care.

Now that she's no longer here
The memories can't be taken away.
So many times they'll bring a smile
And help me through the day.

~ Meetin' Time Again (1989) ~

Written for the United Methodist Women

It's time to go to meetin'
And I'm sure you'll all agree,
That is a very nice place that
We should always be.

We sometimes feel in a dressy mood,
And our best outfit we'll put on,
But other times our slacks will be,
What we'll most likely don.

We talk when we should listen,
But are quiet when we should speak.
Maybe we want to practice,
"Blessed are the Meek."

At last we get our business done,
Sometimes a lengthy affair,
And after much discussion,
We feel like pulling our hair.

Then time for a little fun,
And probably a piece of cake,
That with the help of Mr. or Mrs. Pillsbury,
Someone took the time to bake.

Oh, we're getting kind of old and feeble,

And a little lazy too,

So we just can't seem to accomplish,

What the Lord would have us do.

But after all is said and done,

We try to Christians be,

And thanks be to God through Jesus Christ,

Our faith will set us free.

~ Autumn's Beauty (October 2000) ~

Autumn days are here once more.
The leaves are gently falling down.
Rain caressing each one with tears,
As they slowly touch the ground.

Some still with colors a brilliant hue,
Which always seems a little sad,
To think their days are at an end,
For a life so short they had.

So enjoy each day while it is here,
And do not worry about tomorrow.
God will be with you through days to come,
To give comfort in times of sorrow.

So praise Him for the glory,
Of the earth in beauty crowned.
Thank Him for the eyes to see,
What can nowhere else be found.

~ Trust ~

In the quietness of this hour,
And my soul in need of rest,
I long for peace and contentment,
Secure that God knows what is best.

So I'll trust him for this day,
And for his guiding hand,
I know the love and blessings he gives to us,
Are more than countless grains of sand.

~ **Ocean Waves** ~

Memories of South Carolina
Blue Waves bouncing white caps
To and fro,
Reach out to kiss the shore line,
Then back again they go.

Sometimes they are so gentle,
And hardly make a sound,
But other times they come roaring fiercely,
Angry with all around.

~ Reflections (March 1999) ~

When I look in the mirror,
A face of beauty I like to see,
Instead, I see this old lady,
Staring back at me.

I wonder what she's doing here?
In my house today.
I try and try to talk to her,
But not one word does she say.

It's then I begin to realize that,
She must have come to stay,
So I try to make her welcome,
In every single way.

~ No Vacancy (1999) ~

Hearts of love can give to one,
A tranquil and peaceful life.
But hearts of stone inside of man,
Will always lead to strife.

To look inside ourselves,
And see what others see,
Will always help us understand,
The problem may be "me".

Oh, the devil will cause trouble,
If we let him have his way,
So put a sign inside your heart,
"There's no vacancy today".

We need to always see the good,
Inside of those we know,
For friendships are the joys of life,
As through the years we go.

~ A Babe ~

In a stable so forlorn
One starry night
A babe was born.

His Mother Mary,
So richly blest,
Held him gently,
To her breast.

She rocked him slowly,
To and fro,
He was hers for a time,
But then he must go.

To change hearts of men,
And fill them with love,
That's why he came down,
From heaven above.

~ Caroling We Go (Dec 20, 1998) ~

Written after going caroling with the choir
Songs were ringing in the air,
As to each house we'd go,
Mist and clouds hung everywhere,
Instead of pure white snow.

A little joy we'd try to give,
To each saddened heart,
A prayer in song we'd lift to God,
Then we would depart.

In each car and van,
Laughter would ring out.
Our hearts were full of happiness,
Of that, I have no doubt.

To bring peace and joy to someone,
Comes back to us in turn.
If we could do that always,
God's message we have learned.

~ April Morn (April 2000) ~

The morning sun comes beaming,

When the shades are raised up high,

Making rooms aglow with brightness,

And inward peaks the sky.

Rays of amber across the carpet,

Creating warm spots for my cat,

To curl up in the sunshine,

For her early morning nap.

Sunshine is so welcome,

After dreary winter days.

It fills our hearts with gladness,

In oh, so many ways.

So when the skies are gray,

And you're feeling kinda blue,

Remember that the sunshine,

Will come again for you.

~ Just Thoughts (1998) ~

Everything depends on something or someone
for its growth and beauty. Not just plants,
birds, and insects; but we, ourselves, are
dependent on God and others to reach our full
potential. This was God's plan that we help
and nurture each other. The more we love
the better we can fulfill our destiny.

~ God's Hand (July 2002) ~

God reached down from heaven
To give the world His touch.
He wanted to fill it with beauty
For He loves us so very much.

He gave the trees garments of green,
Flowers of every hue,
Clouds of snowy white
And the sky a mantle of blue.

Little birds fly here and there,
So to each a song He gave.
He gave the bats a place of rest
In a dark and gloomy cave.

He gave the wind to rustle the trees,
The sun to warm the earth,
To animals and bugs both far and wide,
He gave them a time of birth.

He gave tall hills and valleys low,
All throughout the land.
He put deep seas with fishes too,
And countless grains of sand.

So for the many things God gave us,

We should give Him thanks each day.

For all the blessings He bestows on us,

To help along life's way.

~ **My Watch Cat (May 2002)** ~

My big fat cat is lazy
And seldom leaves her bed,
But just before her nightly sleep,
She begs me to be fed.

Then a breath of fresh air,
She sometimes seems to crave,
So out the back door she saunters
Acting so very brave.

Last night out the back walk,
Another cat crouched so very low,
When Callie looked down and spied him,
She slowly waddled to and fro.

That other cat took one look
At that big fat hunk coming near.
His heart began to race in panic,
So he sped off in deepest fear.

Now Callie really knew
That she was in control,
So into the house she came once more,
And headed for her bowl.

She guards me from her window bed
All throughout the night,
And looks to all like a ferocious dog,
Just waiting for a fight.

Caledonia "Callie" Beavers enjoying some sun.

~ **Winter Dawn (1964)** ~

The air was still and cold, and the ground was covered
with white frost like a covering to keep it warm.

The sun was slowly climbing in the sky sending its warming
rays down on the barren earth.

The trees stretched out their branches like long tentacles
reaching for their prey.

No cheerful sound of birds could be heard to break the silence.
It was though everything slept.

But soon the awakening would come! Trees would once more
wave their leaves in friendly greeting.

The flowers would lift their brightly colored garments toward the dazzling sun.

The birds would serenade each living
creature and tell each blade of green, green grass, grow tall!
grow tall!

The world is ever changing. A new beauty always on the way.
So keep your eyes ever watching, the dawning of each new day.

~ God's Hand ~

Did you ever wonder what makes the sky so blue?
What turns the leaves from brightest green
to every golden hue?

Did you ever wonder how rain can turn to snow?
And how a gentle little breeze can become the
fiercest blow?

Did you ever wonder what makes the sun to shine?
Making delightful little shadows of every
shape and kind.

Twas not the will or work of man, these miracles
could achieve.
But God's own hand did create, all things
we must believe.

~ Spring Rain (March 2002) ~

Looking out my window through raindrops
Drenching the parched earth,
Washing things anew
And awaiting their rebirth.

I saw a big fat robin,
So regal in his bright red vest.
He was splashing in the puddles,
So seldom taking rest.

He would pause to listen,
Then he would find his prey.
A wiggling tasty worm
Would feed him for the day.

Spring rains are such a blessing,
Even though the sky is colored gray.
For in our hearts we always know,
Spring flowers are on the way.

~ Early Spring (March 26 2002) ~

On this early spring day,
Thick clouds are overhead.
The wind is playing hide and seek,
Stirring the blossoms in their beds.

The buds are all just waiting,
For a bright and sunny day,
Then they'll all break forth in beauty,
Dressed in their best array.

Little chickadees flit among the branches,
All wearing their black caps,
Stopping to eat some tasty seeds
And keeping a wary eye for cats.

On a day so dark and gloomy,
It might be easy to feel blue,
But in nature we see the promise
Of what God has prepared for me and you.

~ Autumn (2004) ~

The chirp of a cricket,
The shortness of days,
October had come calling,
Sometimes clad in morning haze.

Pumpkins in the fields
Which once were shades of green,
Geese flying high a honking,
These signs of fall are seen.

Some flowers still are blooming,
The goldenrod is so bright,
Stars are shiny and twinkly,
During each longer night.

Mornings now are crisp and cool,
Dew covering each blade of grass
With sparkling little jewels,
But not for long they'll last.

Once again we say goodbye to summer,
The autumn's beauty we're ready to greet,
Trees arrayed in vibrant colors
Enhance each village street.

~ Miracle Of Flight (June 2003) ~

Butterflies, birds, and airplanes
And insects of every kind,
Go through the air a'soaring,
Just look, and you will find.

Butterflies with painted wings of red,
Blue, yellow, and sometimes green,
Flit through days of sunlight,
Their beauty often seen.

Birds of blue, red, and brown,
Their wings spread to catch the air
As they soar among the tree tops,
This all makes a day so fair.

Then man made the airplanes
Which can fly from land to land,
What miracles God has given us
As He guided someone's hand.

We must not forget the insects,
Of course some we could do without--
But still, the wonder of flying,
Given by God, we cannot doubt.

~ **The Old Mill (January 2004)** ~

The old mill stands against the sky,
From my window, framed by a tall old tree
It's really kind of useless now,
But it's rather dear to me.

It's looked down on many a man
That passed by with wagon and horse.
Thinking of those long ago days,
Brings back memories, of course.

That old mill looks down on my back yard,
Where children used to play.
Now it's mostly birds and squirrels
Who chatter through the day.

It could be Kingston's only skyscraper,
As it stands proud and tall,
Its broken windows beckoning,
Owls and bats each Fall.

The memories of this little town,
As it was very long ago,
The peaceful tree lined streets,
I still remember so.

I wouldn't trade this little town
With my home on Elm Street,
For city streets with mansions,
Where my friends, I'd never meet.

The old Mill in Kingston, December 2011.
It is scheduled to be demolished.

~ Life's Pathway (May 2003) ~

As you travel along life's pathway,
Be sure to pause along the way
To see the beauty of the sunrise,
As you start each brand new day.

Last night I saw a tiny rabbit
As he nibbled on clover so green,
Now and then pausing and listening,
For a predator, he may not have seen.

A robin's nest nestled in a tree nearby,
Where a mother will patiently wait,
For that first little peep from her offspring,
As she's fed by her long time mate.

Then a bright red bird lit on my feeder
Seeking a seed before night.
Sudden a big blackbird swooped down
And my beautiful cardinal took flight.

Some frisky squirrels were racing
All through the yard, and around the old elm tree.
Now aren't I glad I took the time
To see what God had prepared for me.

~ The Gift (August 1989) ~

Did I hear someone speaking?
It was not loud or clear,
But I felt a tugging at my heart strings,
And I knew my Lord was near.

It is time that I should tell you,
He seemed to say to me.
I can find a use for you,
Although you may not see.

When a little child is born,
To each a talent I will give,
That they may help all those around,
As long as they shall live.

What I gave to you at that time,
May not seem so very great,
But now you know why I gave it to you,
And it hasn't been too late.

I gave you a flow of words,
That sometimes never cease,
But with this gift you may help someone,
Have a heart of love and peace.

Oh, you'll never write a lovely song,
Or gain heights beyond compare,
But others will to God above,
Lift up your name in prayer.

So cherish this gift I give to you,
No other is quite the same,
For I gave it to you and to you alone,
And all in Jesus name.

~ **Memories (July 2001)** ~

Written in loving memory of my son, Ricky

Where once I was bright and new,
Now I am soiled and worn.
Some of my whiskers are missing,
You see, I'm rather tattered and torn.

Only one button eye has been
Lovingly sewn upon my face.
The other one is still missing,
So my appearance is quite a disgrace.

Little arms once carried me
Up the stairs, then to his bed,
So very carefully he would tuck me
Right up close beside his head.

The comfort I would give him
Chased away the fears of night.
We would cuddle up together
Until the morning brought its light.

In daytime he would play with me;
Sometimes a wagon we would ride.
For the few short years we were together,
I rarely left his side.

I'm just a little panda bear,
Who brought joy to a tiny lad's heart,
And even though he went away,
I'm sure we're never far apart.

The author's son, Ricky, in 1947, age 2, with a stuffed panda.

~ Snowflakes (January 2003) ~

The snowflakes fall so gently,
They hardly make a sound
Creating a scene of beauty
For enjoyment to all around.

While driving to church through a Fairyland,
In a snow globe, we surely were a part,
A happy, blissful feeling
Came from deep inside my heart.

Though icy streets are a hazard
When driving to and fro,
The magic of the snowflakes,
Will soon be gone we know.

We know the snow's a treasure,
A warm covering for the earth,
It's moisture giving life
To all the plants awaiting birth.

Now God will provide all things
When He know that it is time,
So in His hands we place our all,
His gifts are ever sublime.

~ Trust (August 2002) ~

The path is never easy,
That we walk throughout this life.
Many days are filled with happiness,
But others times of strife,

We must place our hand in Gods
And He'll guide us along the way.
We must take the time to talk with Him
Before we start each day.

In times of sickness and in sorrow,
He'll give us strength to bear.
With the peace He puts inside of us,
We will know that He does care.

We need to put our trust
In what He knows is best.
To use the knowledge He has given us,
Then He'll provide the rest.

So thanks to you Dear God,
We know if we wait on Thee,
That You will guide our footsteps,
For our future You always see.

~ A Mama's Love (May 2007) ~

Mama Robin, baby at her side,
Hops back and forth across the lawn all day
The little one, mouth open wide
Is constantly in mama's way.

Most little bugs that mama finds
Go to feed her little one.
Every day from dawn to dusk
It seems her work is never done.

Patiently she keeps him close
To protect him from all harm
God put love in mother birds
And it works just like a charm.

I think some days mama bird
Looks longingly for the setting sun
When she and baby can silently sleep
Now that another day is done.

Soon baby bird will set out on his own
Then mama's legs can get some rest.
But until that glad day is finally here
Mama will do her very best.

~ God's Light (January 2004) ~

It seems I need you more God
On a cold and dreary day.
I sometimes forget the sun still shines,
For the clouds get in the way.

The stumbling blocks of life
Are but clouds to dull our view.
If we look beyond the shadows,
God's light is shining through.

When we look ahead to see His light,
Then our pathways will be clear.
His peace and love will fill our hearts,
As He guides us through each year.

~ Summer Day At Nancy's (July 2001) ~

An old rope swing so proudly hung
From a broad and tall old tree.
How well I remember when I was young,
The joy swinging brought to me.

The gentle sound of splashing water,
Where fish all dressed in gold,
Lived among the lily pads,
In water so pure and cold.

Some busy guineas seemed to chatter,
And the joyful songs of wrens filled the air,
While we swam and basked in sunshine,
Without a worry or a care.

The very proud and handsome peacocks,
All dressed in their best array,
Came through the yard to greet us,
But didn't take time to stay.

The friendly dogs with wagging tails,
They most surely seemed to say,
We hope you spend some time with us
On another bright and sunny day.

~ Dear Old Kingston High (July 2001) ~

Written for the last dance and reunion at Kingston High School before it was to be sold at auction.

The happy shouts of Kingston High,
Are in our memories past.
I sometimes wonder, did we think
It would forever last?

The times we spent with friends
And many teachers too,
Classes, study halls, plays, and music,
Just to name a few.

If we took the time to open books,
We probably did O.K.
But sometimes a caring teacher
Would pass us anyway.

We wonder about the future
Of these dear old ancient walls,
So joyfully filled with voices
Throughout the rooms and halls.

We all have left a part of us,
On the corner of this street,
So may we celebrate our happy times,
As our friends this day we meet.

~ Contentment (March 1998) ~

Skies are often cloudy and gray,
But sometimes the sun peaks through.
In the midst of life's darkest moments,
God will give hope to you.

Peace and contentment
He will place inside your heart,
If to Him you will listen
And your prayers to Him impart.

God will be the answer
To the trials of each day.
Happiness He'll give to you,
If from Him you never stray.

Those far from God will never know
His eternal bliss,
Or feel the brush of angel wings
And the touch of a heavenly kiss.

So put your trust in Jesus,
From Him to never stray,
Then He will guide you safely
All along life's way.

~ That Harley Ride (June 2000) ~

Lynn Strehle took me for a ride on his motorcycle after a choir picnic at his house. I wore his wife's leather jacket and helmet.

Listen my children
And you shall hear
Of my daylight ride,
On that seat at the rear.

All decked out,
In a jacket of leather,
I looked so classy,
In spite of the weather.

Out on the road,
But not very fast.
I wondered how long,
This old lady would last.

Around the corner,
I think on one wheel,
What if I would
"chuck up" my just eaten meal?

Into the town where I was raised,
Not many people were out.
It was a sight to see
Of that, I have no doubt.

When that super Harley,
Pulled back in the drive,
I was happy to note
I still was alive.

Next year we'll try to put on a good show,
And maybe jump over a car.
But heaven's above! Even for me,
That's going a little too far.

~ The Christmas Gift (Dec 1999) ~

Written for my family when the time came
it was hard to buy many gifts.
Mother and Grandmother

The gift I give to you this Christmas,
Could not be found in any store,
I looked and looked along the aisles,
Till I could look no more.

The times of presents wrapped so gaily,
Are in our memories past,
It was such a very happy time,
Then changes came so fast.

I guess I wasn't really ready,
For I feel a little sad,
And then I knew my greatest gift
To you, would yet be had,

Oh, its' wrappings are old and wrinkled,
You see, I've had it for many a year,
But a heart full of love, I give to you,
Because you are so dear.

~ God's Voice (Winter 2000) ~

Snow and ice cover the ground bringing with it
silence, peace and purity to a troubled world.

A time to listen for the voice of God,
And thank Him for His care,
What great a love he has for us,
Each burden He will share.

He doesn't sit upon a throne,
And demand we do His will,
But in His still small voice,
He beckons us, and our beings fill.

~ Spring Rain (April 17, 2000) ~

I awoke this morning,
To the sound of gentle rain.
Each little drop gaily dancing ,
On my window pane.

Puddles by the roadside,
Creating bathing pools for birds,
Chirps and twitters showed their happiness,
Instead of human words.

Trees and bushes awash with brightness,
The smell of lilacs wafting through the air.
Even gray skies bring their blessings,
For days can't be always fair.

Homeward Bound (May 2001)

My boys are homeward bound,
Which brings joy into my heart.
Through many passing years,
In my life they've had a part.

My life has never been the same,
From the time that they were born.
Changing diapers and giving bottles,
Sometimes in early morn.

I've shared their smiles and their laughter,
Told many stories and played games.
I've loved our times together,
How blessed to say their names.

They are no longer boys,
But into young men have grown.
I still feel their love and closeness,
Even when I am alone.

I thank God for their birth,
And for their Mom and Dad,
A family is the greatest gift,
That can on earth be had.

~ Christmas Time Again (Dec 2002) ~

Once again it's Christmas time,
With houses and stores all aglow.
Garlands of red and green, and holly boughs
Dancing as the north winds blow.

Many happy hearts of children
Are full of anticipation as they wait,
For the coming Christmas morning
On that long awaited date.

A tree with balls and twinkling lights,
The gifts piled up so high.
All too soon become a mountain of paper,
Then Mama lets out a sigh.

A table full of goodies
Awaits in a nearby room.
Now a full tummy and a peaceful heart,
It has ended all too soon.

Have we forgotten something?
A reason for the day.
We were all so happy with our gifts
That we didn't take time to pray.

So now we open up our hearts
And give thanks to the Lord above.
We could only celebrate this glorious day,
Because of His abounding love.

~ Guide For Living ~

Each day will be much brighter,
If when you see a need,
You'll reach out with gladness,
To do some little deed.

So put a smile upon your face,
And a song within your heart,
Then you'll find you're helping others,
Without knowing when you start.

If you just reach out to someone,
With a heart so full of love,
You know the angels will be singing
With God in heaven above.

~ Our Little Girl - Baby Grace (2008) ~

A sweet little baby girl with a turned up nose,
Chubby little fingers, and pink little toes,
Entered our lives on an April Day,
We soon could tell from her very first breath,
That she would try to have her way

She loved her mommy and felt secure,
When she was nestled at her breast,
That bond had long been growing,
Before she left her nest.

Oh, we watched and waited for a smile
To adorn her pretty face,
Then she brightened up all our lives
When that event took place,

It's hard to watch and hear her cry,
For we want her to always happy be,
But the life she lives upon this earth,
Only God can see.

Thank you God, for little girls
for us to tend, and love,
may you always give us guidance,
from your home in Heaven above.
With Love, Nanny Beavers, 2008

~ A New Life (May 2011) ~

Elizabeth Rosemarie came into our lives
On an early April day,
She soon would capture all our hearts
In a very special way.

She looked at us with her bright blue eyes
Chubby little cheeks, and a cute button nose.
She really seemed so perfect
From her head down to her toes.

She was a little sleepyhead
And seldom seemed to cry
With tender love from Mommy,
And her little bottom dry.

She's getting a little bigger now
And sometimes we'll see a smile.
I think she wants to say to us
"I'd like to stay for a while."

May she have health and happiness
And feel in her heart our love.
We thank you God, our Father
For this gift from Heaven above.
With Love, Nanny Beavers

Section Three: Additional Photos

Great-Granddaughter, Grace Bennett, Age 2, Spring 2010

Great-Granddaughter, Elizabeth Bennett, Age 7 Months, Fall 2011

Great-Granddaughter, Brianna Bennett, age 14, Fall 2010

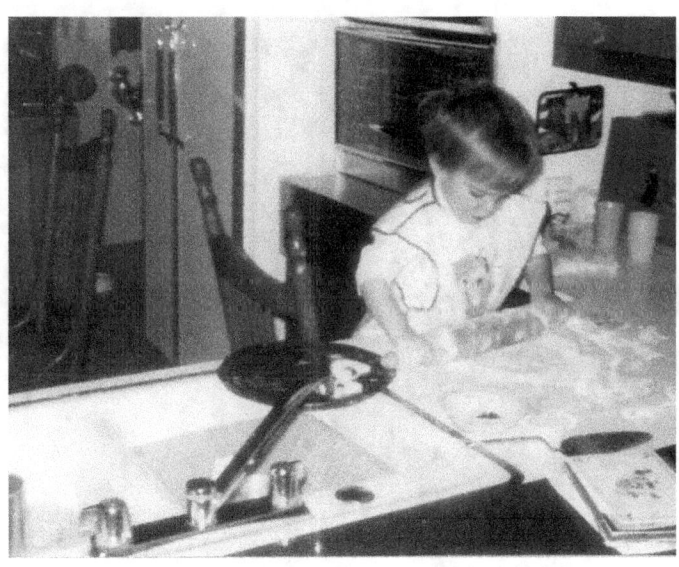

Grandson David Bennett, age 3, rolling cookie dough, 1981

Grandson Jonathan Bennett, age 3, making cookies, 1981

Daughter Jeanne Beavers-Bennett, with husband Barry, 2010